Unlock the Potential of Future Trading: Your Guide to Profits and Success

A Comprehensive Handbook for Beginner Traders to Master Future Trading Strategies and Boost Financial Gains

Lester A. Gray

Bid
Ask
Auto
GBPUSD M15
1.4505
1.00
1.4508
SL/TP

Table of Contents

CHAPTER 1

The Best Platforms and Tools

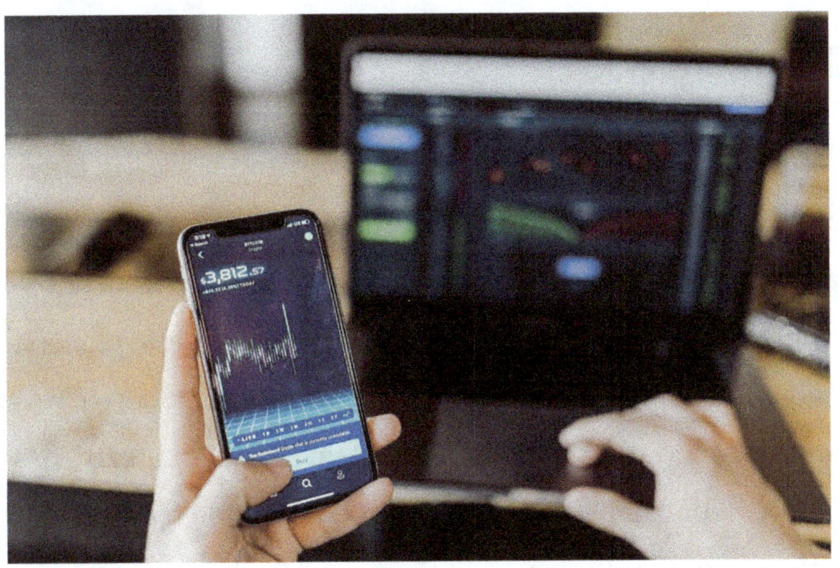

Since the times are quite volatile, choosing a broker for options trading is a very crucial step in order to make good profits. The list of platforms that I have provided here have been selected after extensive research, and they will also provide you with an extensive range of tools that will help you to manage and measure risk and assist you in placing profitable trades. Every platform is unique, and they all have some good points and bad points. Knowing the platform thoroughly is very important before you get started with them, and so, I have tried to provide you with a comprehensive approach.

TD Ameritrade

If you are just a beginner, then TD Ameritrade is really good for you. The platform is also trusted by several expert options traders as well. The reason why they are topping everyone's list is that they offer excellent resources for beginners, reasonable pricing, and lower commissions. It doesn't matter where you are in your journey of options trading; this platform has to provide a lot for everyone. Some of the notable features of this platform are as follows:

- TD Ameritrade had changed its system of commission in the year 2019. It was initially priced at $6.95 for every trade and a $0.75 extra for every contract. At that time, it was quite high as compared to the other brokers. For options trading, the platform only charges a fee of $0.65 for every contract, but this is a very typical rate when compared to other platforms.
- The charting feature of this platform is super good and advanced. In a few clicks, you will have a total analysis of real-time data. There are so many technical studies that you can access for every chart
- The trading tools are endless and impressive. With this platform, it

is safe to say that the only limit is the sky. From replaying historical markets to conducting earning analysis, everything can be done on a single platform. They also have an option to conduct an advanced analysis of the options.

- The earning analysis tool will also help you measure the volatility. In simpler terms, it will make the entire process easier and will also bring clarity so that you can understand everything at once. And do you know what the best part is? With this platform, you will get data from Wall Street analysts at your fingertips.

Tastyworks

If you want to become a frequent options trader, then Tastyworks is the platform for you. The tools that are available on this platform are all about probability, liquidity, and volatility. As per the platforms, most of the trades that are placed on it are derivatives, and thus, their team is more inclined towards designing tools that will be of great help for options traders. Some of the features that you should know about are listed here:

- The process of opening an account on Tastyworks is probably the easiest thing to do. Once that is done, you will have to download the platform. One thing that I love about the platform that you can play around with the platform and check out its features before even funding your account.
- All the tools available on this platform are aimed towards helping you

- to evaluate the probability of profit and also evaluate the volatility.

- One of the key components of the platform is its watchlists, which you can access from the left-hand side of your device's screen. The watchlists are designed to be the same on the downloadable platform, web, and mobile.

- On the right-hand side of the screen, you will get options like alerts, activities, and position details. All the options can be customized based on what you want to see and what you don't. In the middle part of the screen, you will see that there is a trade ticket that remains open so that you can keep track of the transaction that you are constructing even when you are analyzing or charting any trade.

- You will get access to the latest trading ideas from weekly videos on the platform, and there is a huge library of pre-recorded videos as well.

- If you are performing options trades, then it is $0 per leg, for a contract to open a position, it is $1 per leg with $10 per leg being maximum. In order to close, it is $0. If you are performing a trade that has fifty contracts, then it would cost you ten dollars for every leg at the most. In case you choose to close the account, there is no fee.

Robinhood

If you are looking for a completely free platform, then you should check out Robinhood. After all, there is nothing cheaper than getting something for free. If you ask some of the professional options traders, then they will tell you that they do not like the trade handling process of the platform. But if you consider it for beginners, then the platform is really good, especially because it involves less risk. Since there is no amount of trading fee involved, you can basically sell options or buy them safely, and the only amount at risk will be what you invested initially. If you are just starting with options trading and want to you test the water, Robinhood is definitely a good place to start. Some of the features are as follows:

- The best thing about this platform is definitely the fact that it is 100% commission-free.

- You, as an investor, can start right now because there is no minimum account value involved. But yes, if you are purchasing an investment, you have to possess enough money for that. If you are opening a margin account, then the minimal portfolio value that you must have is $2,000.

- The entire process of opening an account on this platform is painless and is highly mobile-friendly. All you need is a few minutes, and you can get it done through the app itself. If you are approved, you will receive a notification within one hour.

E*TRADE

When you are just a beginner, E*TRADE can help you understand how you can improve the returns on your portfolio by trading derivatives. You will get proper guidance throughout your options trading journey. The mobile app is very much intuitive, powerful, and makes way for a smooth workflow. Here are some of the features that you should know about:

- There are two mobile apps available, and the platform has done some wonderful work this year to make its apps even more comprehensive and take the user experience to the next level.

- The Power E*TRADE website has a special tool known as Spectral Analysis, and with this tool, you will be able to assess the maximum amount of loss or profit that you will have for any particular options strategy. You will also get help in learning about the different risk metrics and how they can affect you.

- There is a paper trading function available with this platform that you can implement and test your strategies.

- If you want to place an order, it is extremely easy. There is a system of Trade Ticket, and you can even save the ticket for later. Across every platform, you will get the watchlists.

- In the case of options trades, the platform does not charge any per-leg commission. For most clients, the commissions for every contract are $0.65 whereas, for those who are placing more than thirty trades in a single quarter, the commissions are $0.50 for every contract. If the contracts have a price of $0.10 or even lesser than that, then any kind of fee is waived off.

Charles Schwab

The tools offered by Charles Schwab are robust and promising, and they will provide you with an all-round excellent service. Just like the desktop experience, mobile apps are fully featured. You can also exercise a high level of customizability on the platform. The features of this platform that you should know about are as follows:

- It is one of the very few platforms that will allow you to trade options without any commissions. A competitive contract fee is levied on options—$0.65 for every contract. But the amount is justified when you compare it with other platforms.

- The research offerings of this broker are probably one of the best that you will get. They not only provide earnings reports but also real-time news. There are multiple in-house experts who will provide you with market commentary and a large selection of research reports. You will also get access to a quarterly magazine, and you do not have to pay any extra charge for it.

- A Google Assistant is integrated into the platform, which makes things even easier for users because if you have any market-related query, you can simply ask Google. Apart from this, there is an Amazon Alexa skill too, through which you can not only create a watchlist but also get updates from it.

- Another good thing about the broker is that they do not have an account minimum.

- There are several platforms for this broker. For options trading, they have the StreetSmart Central. You can also exercise mobile trading with them.

TradeStation

If you are planning to take options trading seriously, then TradeStation should definitely be one of your top choices. The TS GO offering of the platform was recently launched, which has zero minimum investment and trading costs. But you can also choose the TS Select plan where you can access the full range of tools, but it will also require an initial investment of $2,000. But there is one drawback, that is, you can access all the advanced tools only when you choose the TS Select plan. The pricing rules can be confusing too but there is no shred of doubt in the fact that the TS Select plan is quite comprehensive. Here are some features of the broker:

- The OptionStation Pro platform of the broker can be availed at free of cost. What is even better is that they have a preview mode through which you can create your own watchlists even on the mobile app, and you can keep track of the trends and charts even when you have not opened an account.

- If you want to get access to the comprehensive research that this broker has, then you will have to go Premium. Once you do that, the TradeStation 10 platform will offer you more than 270 indicators. You can access historical data and then test your strategies by backtesting. And this data is huge because it comprises the daily data for the past ninety years. You will also get intraday data for the past decade.

- There are several free videos, tutorials, and eBooks available from where you can learn a lot about options trading.

Ally Invest

This is quite a low-cost brokerage, and they even have no account minimum. They are backed by Ally Financial. They can also offer you with a universal account management experience along with a website that is very easy to navigate. Some of the greatest strengths of this brokerage are as follows:

- Hey, have excellent customer service. So, if you are a beginner, Ally Invest is something you can rely on because they are so easy to use.

- In order to learn more, you can start with nominal investment, and you don't have to scratch your head about any big minimum fees or balance. You can take your time to learn since there is very low risk involved.

- Placing trades on this platform is a cakewalk, and you can modify settings, view the charts, and also conduct technical analysis like a breeze. There are as many as 117 technical indicators and 36 drawing tools at your disposal.

CHAPTER 2:

When to Trade and When not to Trade

The markets go through different phases and there are times when you will feel like it is difficult to read the market or other times when there are low volumes and high hesitation from market participants making the market evolve in a flat and boring momentum.

DAX future, 5 minutes

For this example, I have used 5-minute candles in order to fit the whole day on one chart. As you can see, the market makes roughly 60 points between its lowest of the day and it's highest of the day, which is not too bad. But how did that happen? A rapid 30 points drop in the morning, followed by a return to opening prices by the end of the morning, and then, 6 hours of long awaiting until a little awakening again at 5pm. Apart from doing mini range trading during these 6 hours, there is not much you can do.

It is difficult to predict how a day is going to be. I am not talking about trends here, but just about price volatility. Is it going to be an active day or a very quiet day? You can't really know in advance. However, there are some hints that you can look for such as previous day's behaviors and chart patterns.

DAX future, one hour

When the market is testing significant levels such as supports and resistances, you can expect some hesitation as no one is willing to buy at the highest and push the market further, until an event or something triggers the market to make a breakthrough or consolidate sharply. When reaching significant levels and testing them, expect the market to test that level before breaking it or reversing.

Another hint to look for market activity can be found in the economic calendars and how the market is reacting to the coming events or news to be announced. The market may enter into a quiet phase, with less participants willing to trade waiting for the news to be released. Some participants will indeed decide to stay on the side, as I will advise you to do next. During this quiet phase, the volumes exchanged could be low, again due to the fact that many day traders don't want to have too many positions opened while facing the risk of high price volatility at the time of the news being released. You should get familiar with the average volume exchanged throughout the day for the product you are trading so that you can assess if the market is being pushed around in low volumes by fewer participants or if indeed there is increased interest.

When scalping, you may want to close all your positions before the news is released because the market might get very volatile on and after the news is being released. While volatility normally serves us, at the time of a news release, the market can move erratically in any direction, come back to where it was before the news went out or set up in a specific direction. What will happen, is that you may have traded in the right direction, but the market went to hit your stop loss first due to price volatility. Now, you may say, let's not put a stop loss in this instance or place it further away, but what happens if the market goes against you and then doesn't reverse in your chosen direction? Placing orders just before the news is released, from my point of view, is just gambling. Don't try to apply logic to the market's reactions to the news either, thinking that if the news is positive the market will certainly go up or the opposite, because it may not happen. The market may already have priced the news with some market participants starting to cash in their profits making the prices go in the opposite direction of where they should logically have gone. When news or a figure is released, you don't have all the information around it. For instance, if crude oil inventories are lower than forecast, is it due to higher oil consumption or lower oil production? What strategies do the market participants have in place? Many factors and many questions for which we don't have all the answers to be able to analyze the news and predict how the market is going to digest the news. Sometimes, following a news publication, the market reacts strongly by going one way, but recovers in the next two hours and resumes its current activity. So, don't try to gamble on the news. With experience; however, you will get to know when important news are likely to have no impact on the market at particular times while they may be strongly scrutinized at other times.

The main macro-economic news that often impacts the markets are interest rates decisions from central banks and their press conferences, crude oil inventories, American employment, inflation figures, GDPs and home sales. Depending on the context they may trigger volatility when released.

You can find calendars with news release dates and times on many websites. I like to use the economic calendar published on investing.com and apply a filter to show the major news.

Economic calendar

As the week is finishing, I look at the following week's events and report them to my computer calendar and save reminders and alarms that go off one hour to 30 minutes before the news release. That way it reminds me not to open any more positions just before a news release, and close existing positions while in positive territory.

Below is a list of additional times when I recommend not trading:

- The first ten minutes after stock market opening. I am talking stock market opening and not future market. During the first ten minutes, the market can move in different ways, not giving us useful readings. Indeed, some participants may be closing positions they didn't manage to close the previous day or for which they had sufficient margin at that time but no longer. Other participants may open or close positions due to their option hedging work and so on. Different traders with different agendas. The first ten minutes may create volatility that again may trigger scalpers' stop losses without giving any opportunity to the scalper.

- The triple witching day: this is the name given to the day when, on a monthly basis, index futures contracts, stock index options contracts and single stock options contracts expire; even quadruple witching day when single stock future contracts adds to this list on a quarterly basis. Triple witching day takes place on the third Friday of the month and quadruple witching day on the third Friday of the month every quarter-end. Volumes become artificially higher due to positions being rolled over to the next contract term. Volatility may also increase as market participants have different agendas, but it may not help the scalper, so I choose to take it easy on these days.

- The last day of the quarter: Some market participants may be at work to improve their balance sheet and quarterly reporting. However, don't start thinking that it will trigger an uptrend because if rising prices may improve the balance sheet of institutional investors, it may have an adverse impact for those with short positions in their books.

- Holidays and festive seasons: during those times, volumes are lower. The market may be in a free-spinning mode or move rapidly in low volumes. If you absolutely want to trade, do it on lower volumes because when institutional investors and big market movers are on holiday the market may not give you the right opportunities to realize good trades.

- Trading after 10pm: Mini DAX and DAX futures are not tradable after 10pm but for the e-mini Dow, CME lets trader carries on their trading on an OTC system via its GLOBEX platform. So, if you really want to trade e-mini Dow non-stop, you can start at midnight on Monday until 11 pm on Friday (these hours can change slightly during the winter and summertime changes). However, trading after 10 pm is not recommended because the volumes are likely to be very low. Focus your energy instead on the US pre-market opening which is at 14:30 CET.

Trading the mini-DAX and DAX pre-market opening

Mini DAX and DAX futures markets open at 7:50 am, one hour and 10 minutes before the stock market opening.

Most of the time pre-market opening is very quiet with low volume transactions. No need to rush to your screen and start trading at 8 am. However, when the market made a strong move the day before, there may be opportunities arising in the pre-market opening. We know that market participants have different agendas, but when the market reacts strongly in one direction, it can put speculators in difficult positions. For instance, if the market went down by 300 points in one day, some long traders may face margin calls meaning they will have to either put more cash in their account or close some of their positions. This will lead to more sell orders being put on the market. At the same time, some sellers may want to cash in and close winning trades. In the first minutes of pre-market opening you won't know how the market will evolve, but you can certainly use the Heikin Ashi candles to perform some trades because after a strong move the day before there is likely to be volatility in the pre-market opening.

DAX, one minute

300 points is a strong intraday move for the DAX.

Quiet pre-market opening has prices that move within a ten to twenty-point range. But here, after a strong move on the previous day, we can expect some volatility.

CHAPTER 3

Understanding Historical Data and Backtesting

There are so many mentors in the business that teach options and stock trading and don't get me wrong there are a lot of very good educators. However, there are also a lot of very bad educators. I was taught how to trade by some of the best traders in the world. My former colleagues at Botta Capital Management stack up against almost any trader out there. I try never to talk poorly about my peers, but I just would be very skeptical of some of the mentors there are.

I have watched so many webinars on trading. I have made money trading in my trading career, but I have also lost money in my trading career. I am proud to say that made money in 11 of my 13 years trading and my total profits are close to $5.5 Million. That doesn't mean as a trader that I haven't gone a day, week, month, or even a year without losing money.

So, when you are watching a webinar and there is a mentor or trader talking about trading, I would ask him three very simple questions:

1. Do you trade a real dollar account?

2. How often do you trade?

3. Can I see your statements from a broker that shows your P&L.

Let's explore these a little bit more in depth before I talk about back testing strategies, because I think that this is a topic that is so important.

Do you trade a real dollar account?

Everyone, I mean, everyone is going to yes to this question. Some mentors teach, but they can't make any money at all trading. Why would you ever want to learn from someone who isn't willing to put their money where their mouth is? The reason that I trade a real dollar account is because I believe that my trading will be profitable. I preach what I believe in and I am willing to put my money where my mouth is. Most traders in a webinar will say, "of course I trade real money." You have no idea how big their position is and to be honest, they do not have to disclose it. Just because a mentor that is giving a webinar is trading a real dollar account does not mean that you can trust them at all. Then we go to question number 2.

How often do you trade?

I have been in this business for a very long time and there is NEVER a best time of the day to trade or best day of the week to trade. Anyone who tells you otherwise has no idea how to trade. When I was on the trading floor, I would try never to ever leave. I risked getting $500 fines for eating on the floor, just so I would not have to leave. Yes, it is true that there is the most action on the opening and closing bell, but that doesn't mean that there isn't money to be made in the middle parts of the trading day. Some of my best trading days happened on holidays or in the middle of the lunch break. I was the youngest trader in the GE pit for a long time, and "the older guys" would go and take lunch for an hour. I would love this because it gave me opportunity.

A broker would walk into the trading pit with a 5,000-lot order of options. Let us say 10 guys showed their size, amount they were willing to trade, of 1,000 each. If they traded everyone would get 500 lot even though they showed 1,000 options because the business would have to be broken up into 10 guys. If there are less people there then the traders would get their quantity, or 1000 each. Other traders in the trading pit were competing against you so the less traders in the trading pit the better. I would always try to stay on the floor all day and used to love when the "older guys" would go get lunch because if there was a good trade that happened that meant more money in my pocket.

Yes, it is true that there are more orders at the beginning of the day, but you never know when a great order will come in. There are people in the business that try to convince others that there is only money to be made on Mondays or at the opening bell but the fact of the matter is that this is not true and a great trader is always in front of the computer screen trying to make money. If I miss a trade that I could have made $200 or $300 during the day I get mad at myself. Moral of the story, do not trust a trader that isn't trading at all times of the trading day.

The final question is about a mentors P&L. My clearing firm was Goldman Sachs and I used to get printed statements from them every single day and not once did I get a statement that was an excel document. Anyone can make up an excel document where it shows them being profitable. If someone giving a webinar shows you a excel P&L statements or does not show you a P&L statement run for the hills. This is the first time in 6 years that I have lost money trading, but it happens. This is the rollercoaster of a trading so if you think you have what it takes you must have a strong stomach.

The next point I want to make is on backtesting.

I like to compare trading to sports so let us look at it like this. If I told you the Chicago Cubs were 3-0 on Monday afternoon games when they started a left-handed pitcher and the other team had a player with the last name of Smith, is this strong enough of a signal to bet on the game? The answer is no. Yes, it is true that the Chicago Cubs are undefeated on Monday afternoon games when they start a left-handed pitcher and the other team has a player with the last name of Smith. However, this does not show a meaningful relationship.

How about if I told you that AAPL goes up every Monday when it is down on Friday in the month of October, but the date has to be an even date not an odd date. Would this be an actionable trading idea? The answer is no. There are too many variables.

What if I told you that 8 of the last 10 times AAPL had earnings the stock rallied from the close of the day before earnings to the next day. Is this an actionable trading idea? The answer to this is yes, it makes sense, AAPL has low expectations on earnings and the stock moves higher because it has a good quarter. Let us know to take these concepts and move them to the idea of backtesting.

In backtesting, we should always ask ourselves these questions:

1. Does the strategy make money in the past?

2. Does why it is profitable to make sense?

As we talked about there is historical volatility and implied volatility. The historical volatility shows us how much a stock has moved over a given period of time and the implied volatility shows us how much the market makers are implying the stock can move in the future. The historical volatility helps us imply the future but can never predict the future. Just like a relationship, we can use the past to help to predict the future, but we never know what the future will bring. Past performance is not indicative of future results. However backtesting can help gives us some useful insights, as long as we know what we are looking at.

Let us talk about the game of Craps. Once a number is hit, a player can make money if any number is rolled with two dice except for 7. The house wins with 7 and you might ask yourself why this is. It is because a 7 will show up with two dice more than any other number and that is why it is the houses' number.

CHAPTER 4

Proven Futures Trading Strategies

One thing to remember, is, that even if you buy and sell futures contracts in commodities, you do not actually take delivery of the underlying commodity. You would close out your contracts before the delivery date.

Let us take a simple example and relate that to a futures contract. You saw a house for sale for $300 000. You believe that in the next year its value will appreciate by about 10% but the downside is you don't have enough money to buy the house outright, so you decide to put down a deposit of $30 000. One year later the property has appreciated in value, as expected, by 10% and is now worth $330 000. You decide to sell the property and make a profit of $30 000. Your initial investment was $30 000, and you sold the house at a profit of $30 000, which gives you a 100% profit on your investment.

Commodity trading works very similarly. Let us take an example. You have been analyzing the corn market and you expect the prices to increase, so you decide to buy the September contract which is presently trading at $2.40 per bushel. There are 5000 bushels in a corn contract. You pay a $500 deposit or margin as required by the exchange.

After four weeks the price has increased to $3.40 a bushel, as expected. This means the contract value is now $3.40 X 5000 = $17000. You bought the contract at $12000 ($2.40 X 5000) four weeks ago and you made a profit of $5000 ($17000 -$14000). The return on your investment of $500 is 1000% in just 4 weeks.

You can also make profits when market prices drop. Let us say you anticipate a drop in the soybeans price from its current level of $5.00 per bushel. There are also 5000 bushels in a soybean contract. You decide to sell one September contract at the current level. You pay a $1000 deposit or margin. Six weeks later the price has dropped considerably, as expected, to $3.50 per bushel. You decide to close your position and take your profits. You do this by buying a contract to offset the contract you sold six weeks earlier. The difference between the price you sold, and the price bought back is your profit. $25000($5.00 X 5000) – $17500($3.5 X 5000) = $7500 profit for an investment of $1000. 750% profit in six weeks.

Selling Short—How does it work?

How can one make money when the market is dropping? This is something that happens around us every day of our lives. Let us say you are a car dealer and you sell brand new cars. The factory-supplied you with a couple of cars on consignment that you can display on your showroom floor and you do not have to pay for them right away because the factory allows you some time to sell them. After a while, you sell one of the cars for $50 000 and now you have to pay the factory, but only $30 000, which is the cost price to you that leaves you with a profit of $20 000. What did you actually do? You borrowed the car from the factory and sold it to your client at a higher price than the factory charges you and that way you made money. You sold first and bought it later. When we sell futures, we do the same thing, we sell high because we anticipate the market will trade down and we can buy back or close our position at a lower price and make a profit. Just like the car dealer.

There Must Be Risks?

With any business you have risks. When you open a business, you have to invest huge amounts of capital upfront to set up your business. You have to rent offices, buy stock and pay salaries, etc. before the first customer walks through your door. You have no idea how many customers will walk in or whether you will generate enough business to even recover your capital expenses. With the speculative markets it is the same but how you manage your risk will determine your success.

Let's compare the stock market with the futures market, you can diversify your risk in the stock market by investing in different non-correlated stock and under normal circumstances, it will work well but sudden political changes or news regarding the economy can affect all share prices overnight, even if you did spread your investments across a number of companies, all your profits can be wiped in extreme situations, as we have seen in recent years.

Comparing this to futures markets where you can spread your investments across a diverse range of commodity markets like corn, silver, oil, sugar, wheat or cotton, it is impossible to imagine any situation affecting all these markets at the same time. Economic disasters, droughts, war, floods, and political events will always happen and they also affect certain commodity markets, but spreading your investment not only minimizes your losses but also puts you in a position to benefit from any price move, whether it is up or down. For example, sudden floods hit the wheat crop, causing shortages and price rises, or bumper crops cause the prices to fall, but you are well-positioned to benefit from any price move, up or down. Commodity traders are only looking for trends, whether it is up or down.

It is this ability to diversify your investment across a number of uncorrelated markets and make enormous profits on short term investments over a few weeks that makes futures trading so much more attractive and less risky than the stock market.

Trading Like Professionals

Who makes the most money in any industry? The professionals do. The reason for this is that they do all the necessary research, get all the necessary training, stick to the rules of their trading systems like magnets and never take short cuts. Can you imagine what will happen if, for example, Doctors decide that certain techniques they have learned to use at university are unnecessary when performing an operation and use their own untested procedures? I do not think we would trust them to operate on us because we have no guarantee of the outcome. The reason why we trust Doctors today is that we know they are disciplined and well trained and know exactly how to treat us in a given situation and they will never take short cuts.

You might ask me what this has to do with commodity trading. If you want to be successful in commodity trading, you will have to act like the professionals and always stick to the rules and your trading system and never take short cuts.

Trading Methods

There are basically two types of trading methods:

Fundamental Trading

This is where you have to do research into the markets in which you want to trade, read the daily press reports on weather conditions, study information like supply and demand figures, agricultural reports and economic news, etc. This takes up an excessive amount of time and money and is mainly used by large institutional investors with the necessary resources to do all the research.

Technical Trading

With this method, you make use of charts to analyze the movement of the markets, also known as Technical Analysis. It is much more suited for the small trader. It does not require having to make decisions based on a lot of subjective information.

Technical Analysis

You have embarked on a very exciting journey into the profitable world of technical analysis. I will walk you through the core concepts of charting and show you how to time your trades with precision.

Who uses technical analysis?

Speculators like us who are looking towards making big profits, Professional fund managers' very livelihood depends upon making other people rich, Hedgers or commercials are the people who actually own the physical commodities. In short, all market participants who demand a professional edge. This tells us only one thing—if the professionals use technical analysis, it must be very important, before we get too really good stuff, it is important to understand why technical analysis works.

CHAPTER 5

Trading Strategies in the Bear Market Economy that Really Work with the Support of a Final Technical Analysis

If a bear market starts with a severe, rapid decline, everyone is aware that something bad just happened. At first, some investors will view the correction or crash as a buying opportunity and not as a bear market.

As an investor or trader, you should be more concerned with what is happening rather than why it happened. It is more important to pay attention to the clues rather than get caught up in the emotions. It is almost always impossible to predict crashes. A major international financial crisis in Asia or Europe, a credit crunch, a spike in interest rates, a currency crisis, a weak economy, a plunging dollar, a mistake by the Fed, or the start of what appears to be a major war—any of these can cause a crash. One seemingly harmless event might be the catalyst, but in a crash, like a house of cards, the whole deck falls down (i.e., the vast majority of stock prices tumbles).

Now the market is in a hard selloff, perhaps 10 percent or more. Do not agonize if you didn't get out before this. The important question is what to do now. You must decide whether you should sell quickly to avoid more losses or hold and hope that the market rebounds. Hope is not a good emotion to have during a crash (or a bear market). In fact, hope has no place in the vocabulary of any investor or trader.

The market often gives those still holding long positions a window of opportunity to get out of a bear market before the real damage is done. Many people miss this chance. Instead of limiting their losses and taking a relatively small hit, they do nothing until losses exceed 30 or 40 percent.

It would be nice to know when a 5 percent loss will turn into a 50 percent disaster, or when that 5 percent loss will become a 3 percent gain a few days later. Unfortunately, there is no foolproof way to tell every time.

The best antidote against losing money in a downturn is to be aware of when a market is getting dangerous. You must always be aware of your market environment. If a 3 to 5 percent pullback occurs during a strong bull market, do not be too alarmed. If that same pullback occurs during a sideways market or a bear market, alarm bells should be going off.

As the bear market continues, even disciplined investors become nervous and wonder if they should sell. The scary part is that no one can predict what is going to happen. Investors start worrying about worst-case scenarios.

As the market keeps dropping, some experts will continue to suggest that you buy on the dip. Do not listen to them. Conversely, others will claim that the market is headed for a massive crash. Do not listen to them, either. React to facts and figures, to the information you get from your charts and from your key indicators — not emotions.

Often during a bear market, many retail investors start off by buying and holding. As the market continues to fall, some of them panic. Although they were determined to hold on to their stocks and mutual funds, once losses reach 50 percent or more, they can no longer take it. As the market continues to fall, the final stage occurs — capitulation: mass panic by sellers.

This is the point when investors collectively throw in the towel and get out, accepting any available price for their holdings. The pain becomes so great that they sell all of their positions, right at the bottom! In fact, one of the reasons that a bear market often ends so violently is the huge wave of people who suddenly sell. As mutual fund redemptions increase, and stocks are sold in a panic, stock prices are driven lower and lower.

Sadly, at this stage, almost all asset classes (bonds, commodities, emerging markets, etc.) fail, so there is no safe haven other than cash. When everything falls at once, most diversification formulas are nearly worthless.

Because retail investors are selling their mutual funds, money managers must sell stocks. This pressure adds to the stock market's woes and prices fall even further. It is a mad dash towards an exit door that is slowly closing. It is not easy to get out when everyone else has the same idea. At this point, people want out of the market at any price.

If you are on the sidelines watching, that final wave of capitulation is a signal that the market is nearing bottom. No one wants to unload a portfolio close to the bottom, but many do, because they are afraid their stocks and mutual funds are going to zero.

Others, who have held tightly to their investments on the way down, decide to keep holding no matter what. Many feel like sitting ducks. (All they can do now is hope that their investments come back to even.)

You may have taken some losses (change that to, you did take some losses), but if you can get out of a bear market with less than 10 percent in losses, you're using a successful strategy. By the time, the market stops falling, 10 percent losses will seem like a gift.

Eventually, there are fewer and fewer sellers. Guess who steps into the market now. If you said buyers, you are right.

As the sellers slowly disappear, the buyers come in looking for bargains, which establishes a base for the next rally. One day, the bear market really ends, and the financial pain is reduced. All of the panicked sellers stop selling, and a bottom is created. This bottoming process can take a long while.

Those who lost money during the bear market are counting their losses and deciding what to do next. More than likely, the market will go sideways for a lengthy time period before turning into another bull market.

There are usually clues that a bear market is on its last legs. Once again, you have to be alert to these clues, because you want to enter a bull market early and ride it as long as you can. Doing that can be a tremendously profitable experience.

Here are market indicators at bear economy to take note:

1. Moving Averages: Briefly, if the S&P 500 or other major indexes rise and stay above their 50-day, 100-day, or 200-day moving averages, this is a bullish signal. As you know, there are no guarantees, because no indicator is perfect, but it is an important clue. In fact, if the S&P 500 rises above its 200-day moving average, that is a significant signal to many investors that the market is making a strong comeback. Even if you don't pay attention to other indicators, pay attention to the mighty 200-day moving average.

2. MACD: When MACD crosses above its 9-day signal line or moves above the zero line (and stays above it), this is a bullish signal. Nevertheless, always confirm with other indicators and your own analysis before buying or selling. As you know, no signal is 100 percent reliable.

3. RSI: RSI tells you whether the market index is overbought or oversold. If RSI falls below 30, that is a signal that the market is in oversold territory.

(Similarly, when RSI rises above 70, that signals an overbought market.) Unfortunately, RSI can remain overbought or oversold for long time periods before the index reverses direction. Nevertheless, it's useful in pointing out when the market is getting a bit extreme.

4. Chart Patterns: If the bear market is really coming to an end, when you look at a chart you might see patterns such as a double bottom. That occurs when the market does not break below major support levels and then reverses direction (twice). The second time it holds support, it forms what looks like a "W," which propels the market higher.

To summarize, market indicators are powerful tools, but they are only tools. They do not provide secrets and are only a method to help determine which way the financial winds are blowing. Every brokerage firm, as well as major financial websites will have charts and indicators. Again, use indicators in conjunction with your own observation and analysis.

How to deal with the bear economy?

Many people fear bear markets because they cause so much financial and psychological damage. Nevertheless, during a downturn, there are strategies you can use to take advantage of it. Instead of being scared, you can profit. Don't be scared – be prepared!

If you can identify a bear market in its early stages, you can make money, and sometimes a lot of money. In fact, some astute traders do best during chaotic times, when the market is on the way down and large numbers of players are panicking. Although the vast majority of people hate corrections or bear markets, if you are willing to own bearish positions, you can prosper.

Once you have confirmed that a bear market has begun, you have two choices: You can flee (exit) or you can fight (own bearish positions).

Flee: You make no attempt to profit from a falling market. Your goal is to exit long positions, protect your assets, and wait for an appropriate time to reinvest.

Fight: You hold positions that prosper when the market declines (such as selling short or holding inverse ETFs). Profiting from a falling market is simply another investment strategy that every investor should learn.

Fleeing from a Bear Market

Fleeing from a bear market is an easy strategy. You simply sell your stocks and move to cash. As long as you aren't selling in the later stages of a bear market, moving to the sidelines is a wise choice. Cash may not provide substantial returns; however, your goal is not to earn profits, but to avoid danger. Do not ignore tax consequences, but avoiding losses is more important than worrying about how much you pay in taxes (talk to a tax professional, though, before taking any action).

Fighting with a Bear Market

Instead of running away from an approaching bear market and hiding in cash, you can profit from the downturn. There are a number of strategies you can adopt. Here are a few ideas, although the strategy you choose depends on your risk tolerance and financial goals, as well as your comfort level.

CHAPTER 6

Forex Trading Merits and Demerits

Forex trading has many favorable aspects, but just like every other trading activity, it has a downside. Every trader that seeks to enter the trade system must assess the advantages and disadvantages of foreign exchange before they make a decision in the appropriateness and attractiveness of the market.

Merits of forex trading

Forex exchange has a large number of advantages regardless of the risks; therefore, it makes an attractive and lucrative activity. The advantages include:

Leverage

Leverage provides traders with substantial opportunities for them to trade and make profits. Access to leverage largely determines the difference between small profits and large ones. In the foreign exchange market, there are more resources for leverage than other markets and depending on the location from which a trader is working from one can get the resource they need. A trader may be able to access a margin that supports a leverage of 100:1 or more for the initial capital.

Fast returns

The foreign exchange market moves very fast, and the liquidity is very deep. When the speed, liquidity, and high leverage are combined in the forex market, they create high opportunities for the trader to make exponential profits in the trade more than other markets. In some other markets, the traders have to wait for very long and still get limited returns.

Easy short selling

In some other markets, short selling may require a trader to borrow assets and get exposed to risks, but in the forex exchange, short selling currencies have a simpler process. Foreign exchange works in a way that the trader buys one currency while selling the other. In other words, the currencies are traded in pairs. Traders speculate the inclines and declines of different currencies; therefore, sell the losing currency and buy the winning pair without involving a borrowing process.

Liquidity

Because the forex market is the largest market in the world by volume, there are many participants; therefore, liquidity for trading is ample especially for the major currencies. Liquidity allows the traders to buy and sell the currencies quickly at any time; there is a flow of traders in the market. A large number of participants in the market enable the trader to transact extremely large orders of currencies without diverting the prices too much. Liquidity reduces the chances of price anomalies and manipulation, and as such, the spreads become tighter leading to efficient pricing. A trader does not have to worry about the stagnant prices during the afternoon and high volatility during the opening and closing which constantly affect the equity markets. In the forex market, a trader can observe similarities in the patterns of volatility (low mid and high) apart from times when major events occur.

Lack of central exchange

Keeping in mind that the forex exchange market operates globally, there is no central regulatory or centralized exchange. The market operates as an over the counter although central banks occasionally interfere with the operations as needed in order to regulate it. However, it is very rare for the central banks of any other authority to intervene unless under extreme conditions. The decentralization and deregulation of the market ensure that the traders are safe from sudden surprises. Many of the other security markets are centralized for example the equity market. When a company trading in the equity market suddenly reports losses or declares a dividend, the prices suddenly react to the information. Regulated markets also have higher chances of insider information compared to forex markets.

A variety of pairs to trade

There are eight major currencies traded in the forex market, and they result in 28 major currency pairs that one may choose from. A trader can select any pair and easily switch from one to the other.

Low capital requirements

A trader can start trading in the forex market with a low amount of initial capital because of the tight spread in relation to pips. In some other markets, one may not be able to trade without a large amount of capital. To ice the low capital cake, forex exchange also has a margin trading and leverage factor.

Technical strategy

Many traders venturing into bonds and equity have to delve deep into the financial and fundamental state of the bonds or share issuer in order to confirm that there are chances of making a profit. However, the forex market, traders do not have to dig too deep; all they need is to study the price charts. Technical analysis of forex market price charts helps the traders identify their entry and exit points. However, they may choose to combine technical and fundamental analysis when selecting a trade.

While fundamental analysis requires one to get detailed background information about the assets of the issuer and the financial health and prospects, Technical analysis requires one to watch the trends and histories of the market; therefore, getting clues on the demands and supply of the currencies.

No insider price manipulation

Many markets such as stock markets and bond markets can be influenced by information held privately by some investors and insiders who have interests in the assets. This is because most of the markets are centralized. Foreign exchange markets are not centralized; therefore, they cannot be easily manipulated by people who have insider information.

In most cases, the only holders who can access insider information in the forex exchange are central bank authorities or government officials, and they are usually under a lot of intense scrutiny from the public and the private sectors. As such, the foreign exchange market is one of the most transparent markets one can trade-in.

Few commissions and fees

Traders get charged Pricey commissions and hidden trading fees when dealing with bonds, equities mutual funds and other kinds of instruments. This makes trading very expensive and reduces the profits of the trader. In forex trade, the costs of trading are determined by the bid-ask price only. The spread price is the difference between the bid and the ask price which is clearly published in real-time by the brokers. As such, a trader does not have to worry about eliminating breakage overheads. This aspect makes Forex exchange more advantageous to trade-in.

Simple tax Rules

In many other markets, the traders have to keep track of their trading activities both in the short term and the long term in order to report taxes. However, Foreign exchange trading is in most cases subject to a simpler tax rule; therefore, making tax calculation very easy.

Automation

Technology advancements have made it easy for forex traders to trade with utmost ease. The trade has adapted well to automatic trading strategies, and with some training, a trader can reap the benefits of the available moves. A trader can set up programming entry, automated trades, limit prices and stop-loss before he/she even makes a trade. The trader may also instruct the trading platform to transact when there are certain price movements or market conditions.

When a trader identifies a well revised automated strategy, he/she may have the chance to take advantage of the daily swings in the market without having to put all their efforts in keeping up with the movements in the market.

Suits different trading styles

Trade in the forex market happens at all hours of the day, Monday to Friday; therefore, enabling a trader to work at their own convenience. This schedule is very beneficial especially for short term traders because they take positions over a limited timeframe (a few hours or even a few minutes.). Some traders prefer to trade during off hours. Off hours refer to the times when one trade zone is not so active, and the other is active. For example, when it is daytime in Australia, it is nighttime on the east coast of the United States. If a trader is based in the US, he may trade AUD during the business hours in the US because the prices are quite stable and little development is expected to occur during the off hours for UAD. The traders who prefer off-hours trade adopt the strategies of high volumes and low profits because they have a little profit margin. The low-profit margin results from the lack of developments in the particular currency. Off-hours traders; therefore, try to compensate the low-profit-margin with high volume trades during the low volatility period. Other trading styles allow the traders to hold positions for a longer time — days to several weeks.

Demerits of forex trading

Although trading may appear easy at first sight, there are challenges that make it hard for the traders. In some cases, the challenges can have serious adverse effects on the trader.

Volatility

All markets show volatility at one point or another. The forex market is not excluded from volatility. Forex traders are exposed to volatilities at times, and if the effects are negative, the trade will be unprofitable.

Forex can disadvantage small traders

In a day, the foreign exchange market can transact up to but not limited to $5 trillion dollars. That huge amount of transaction is usually done by the main layers such as hedge funds, banks, and other larger institutions. These major players have access to a lot of capital, technology and also information that might give them an upper hand while making decisions; therefore, they are naturally advantaged. To some extent, these major players can influence the movement of prices in the market.

On the other hand, a small trader will have to stay alert and use the latest information in the best way possible because the forex market is very fast-moving. The reality of small traders being disadvantaged is evident in almost all markets, but the forex exchange market is highly affected.

The forex market is not regularized, and it is dominated by brokers. The fact that there are many brokers makes it hard to have full transparency. A trader is competing against professionals, and he/she may not have a say in how the trade order gets fulfilled. The trader may also not get a good price, and he/she will only have access to the quotes provided by the selected broker. The best course is to deal with the brokers who are under the broker regulators. Although the market is not regulated, the actions of the brokers are.

The complex process of price determination

The rates in the forex markets are determined by multiple factors such as global politics, economic status, among others. Some of these factors can pose challenges in analyzing and quantifying; therefore, a trader can have a hard time drawing reliable conclusions on the trade. To a large extent, forex trading relies on technical indicators (Mathematical calculations based on volume, price or open interest of securities). Technical analysts analyze historical data and use the indicators to predict the price movements in the future. If a trader gets the predictions wrong, he/she will incur losses.

Lighter regulatory protection

Many traders and investors have a list of securities they can choose to trade in, and they prefer to act on trades that are swift and have transparent pricing. For most well-known securities, trading takes place in on formal exchanges constituting of large institutions that set the regulations and are regularized to guarantee an active market, a flow of assets and robust supply/demand balance.

Foreign exchange market is not centralized and does not have a fixed oversight regulation. Therefore, it is an over the counter market. The main challenge with over the counter markets is that the trader will have to conduct a due diligence investigation to confirm the reputation and trading practices of the brokers before opening an account with them. Again, lighter regulatory protection might put the trader at risk because; depending on the country that one is trading in, he/she may have no way of getting compensated if he/she feels that the broker gave unfair treatment.

CHAPTER 7

Control Your Emotions like A Pro – A Step-by-Step Guide

Since trading options is mostly about short time periods, most people have this idea that the prices of options are not going to fluctuate much in that time. But that is wrong, and you need to rethink if you are thinking along those lines as well. If you study past data, you will see that options trading witnesses a lot of fluctuations in price even if it is over a short period of time. So, if you think that options trading means your money will stay protected, then I have to tell you that you are wrong. Of course, people lose money in options trading, just like investing directly in the stock market. But that does not mean you have to be happy about the fact you are losing money because you will feel low and you will start panicking—that is the NORMAL reaction. But you have to learn how to keep your emotions in check.

You need to learn how to remain calm and observe your emotions from a distance instead of giving in to them. Slowly, you will learn how you can stick it out so that you can see whether or not you get any good returns in the future before the expiration date. Options trading can really be a financial roller coaster. You cannot invest in options with the mentality of a Warren Buffet investor because options do not appreciate in the same manner. A little bit of study would reveal that options increase on a percentage basis, and their movement is way faster than any other type of investment.

For example, if a person has multiple contracts in his/her possession and is trading them all, then they might incur simultaneous losses and profits of $500 each over the course of a few hours. But technically speaking, do not confuse options traders with day traders because they are not, but your mindset should be slightly like that of a day trader if you want to make it big in options trading.

In this chapter, I am going to show you how you can control your emotions even when you are on this rollercoaster ride of options trading.

Getting Started

As a beginner, you will have a tendency to jump into the market right away and begin your journey as a trader. But before you do that, let me remind you of some of the things that are crucial for you to learn. I cannot stress enough on the fact that a good and proper understanding of the basics of options trading is going to get you far in your journey. You also should learn about the different types of options that are present in the market so that you know what you should pick. I know that I have probably told you all of this before, but I am reiterating this for one simple reason, and that is—this is the golden rule about being a top trader. The more you enhance your knowledge about investing, the more will be your chances to get success.

Once you have gone through all the basics and understood them carefully, you will have a clear picture in your head about what you are getting yourself into. The next step is to find your motivation and always hold tightly to it because, in trading, beginners tend to lose that motivation very fast. You need to ask yourself exactly how much money you think about making. The figure will vary from person to person, and although there is no limit to this, you should still be realistic about it. No one becomes a billionaire overnight. You should also ask yourself how you plan to spend or use that money once you have earned it. This is where you are going to find your motivation because you are setting goals or you have some dreams that you want to fulfill, and so you will try your best to make those dreams come true. When you are in the thick of the trading, this motivation is going to keep you going and also help you stay focused on the trade.

When you have the trading plan ready, it will constantly tell you about the things that you should achieve in a trade. Some of the common things that are included in a trading plan are — your goals, your idea of what is going to happen, the strategies that you want to use, and any other note or guideline that you think might be of use to you. All of this together is going to make you successful. You will be putting yourself into a risky endeavor if you start trading without having this plan ready.

Never Make Emotional Decisions

As you must have understood by now that options are very volatile in nature, and depending on certain stocks, it can get really very volatile. There are so many beginner traders who come into options trading but then become emotional because it is not what they thought it would be. And this is exactly what I am talking about. This approach will not do any good to you, and that is why prior research is necessary to know the waters you are stepping into.

In most cases, people exit at the wrong time just because they became emotional and overwhelmed during the trade, but only if they had stayed a bit longer or if they had made their exit a bit early, they would have been able to make a lump sum profit. If you are trading options, your worst mistake would be to make any sudden moves. That is why a trading plan is so necessary so that you can have all the rules at hand when you need to exit or enter a trade. And all you have to do is stick to those rules.

The tides in the financial market keep changing, and if you want to navigate them like a pro, then active monitoring is important. There will come a time when you will feel like giving in to your behavioral impulses, but you have to stop yourself right there and take a step back to analyze the situation in front of you. The market ups and downs can easily make you start practicing emotional buying and selling if you are not careful. And the usual trend shows that whenever the market is good, investors have the tendency of piling into investments and then they sell at the bottom. This is mostly because of the fear and hype generated by media.

There are several theories that have been proposed about investor behavior because it is something that is being studied extensively. But if we look at the real-life situation, you will understand that trading can bring about stress, and in situations of extreme stress, it is quite common for rational thinking to be clouded by the investor's psyche. The stress can not only be a result of panic but also euphoria. That is why I have told you time and again that the approach towards investing should be realistic and rational. Never underestimate risk management because every investment has its own risks, and if you do not gauge those risks, then you are the one who will be at a loss.

There are so many non-professional investors in the market who actually use their hard-earned money for trading just because they think they are going to receive a huge return. But sometimes market developments can lead them to lose their money, and it is very painful indeed. All of this leads to extreme stress and that stress, in turn, can lead to second-guessing every step. That is why you need to identify what your risk tolerance is so that you do not end up making emotional decisions when these risks become unbearable for you.

Be a Bit Math-Oriented

If you are not good with numbers or if you are shy about it, then you are not going to do well in options trading. This is because it is entirely a game of numbers. But don't get me wrong, I am not asking you to go to some renowned university to get a degree in mathematics or statistics. You can read a bit by yourself and get a grasp on the basic concepts because a little bit of knowledge about statistics and probability will do you good in the long term and make you better than the others in the world of options trading. To be honest, I don't know how you are going to get to the top if you do not know the basics of statistics. The core of options trading will always have some Maths in it, and you cannot go around it in any way.

Also, when you are math-oriented, you will have a better understanding of the market, and you will see options in a different light. You will learn to analyze the situations and markets before going all-in with your capital. This, in turn, will also make strategizing an easier process.

Maintain Trading Journals

When you have a trading journal, keeping track of your trade becomes way easier. Your brokerage statement is not going to include everything, whereas your trading journal will have all those details, making it easier for you. It will also remind you of the mistakes you made in a certain market condition. Do you know how this is going to benefit you? If that same market condition were to repeat itself, you know exactly what strategy you will not be using, and this will help you not to make the same mistake again. You can also keep track of every time you became emotional and what triggered you. This is will not prevent you from becoming emotional, but it will remind you of the loss you incurred, and this probably will help you get a grip on yourself.

When you record your trades and make notes in your journal, you get a clear picture of the situation you are in. Yes, sometimes, that picture can be bad, and this does not mean that you have to back out. A losing record is simply when you have to find out where you are going wrong and why you are not making profits from the trade. All of this will become easier because you have written your steps in the trading journal. And then all you have to make is adjustments.

Maintain a Disciplined Approach

You must be wondering what I mean by a disciplined approach. Well, I simply mean that don't invest your money in options just because you have a feeling about them, or you think they make you feel good. No! That is just gambling and nothing else. Before investing, you have to perform thorough research. You have to pay attention to how the stocks performed in the past years and also be aware of what its recent history is.

Also, most beginners do not revisit their trades once they have closed it. Don't do that. Even if you have made a profit from a trade, revisit it at some other time to see if there were any improvements that could have been made and then make a note of that because it will help you in your future strategies when similar market conditions arise.

You should never blame the market for anything because it is simple blame-shifting and nothing else. If anyone is responsible for the losses you incurred, then it is you. That being said, you do not have to beat yourself up emotionally if you made a loss. You have to learn from it, get up, and not repeat the same mistake again.

CHAPTER 8

The 11 Commandments of Swing Trading

Some of the most experienced swing traders of 2019 like to focus on what has become known as the 11 commandments of swing trading. Popular trader, Melvin Pasternak, developed this list and discusses it after his trading classes.

Make Sure to Have Long Strengths and Short Weaknesses

There are two periods that you should be looking for when you are taking on a trade. The first period is known as bull and the second period is known as bear. You need to be able to identify these periods when you get into the market because this will let you know what the market conditions are like for that time. When you look at the bull market condition, you are looking at an increasing market. The stock trends are on an upward trend, which they have been on for a good period of time. This proves that the levels of the economy are high, and you should spend your time looking for longer trades.

When the market's condition is focused on bearishness, this means that the stocks are on a downward trend. The prices of stocks are dropping, and many traders believe that this is the spiral that they will see in some stocks for a period of time. Bear conditions happen when the economy isn't doing very well. This is normally during points of economic recession and when unemployment is high. When you notice the bear conditions, you will want to focus on short trades as this will limit your risk of loss, especially if the downward trend continues.

The Overall Direction of the Market and Your

Trade Should be aligned

This is one reason research is important. You not only want to research when you are starting your swing trade profession, but you also want to continue your research. In fact, every day that you sit down in front of your desk is a day that you will be doing research. One of these reasons is because you have to make sure to research and analyze every stock. This will help you determine whether you should purchase the stock or not. When you are focusing on your research for a particular stock, one of the main focuses should be does the stock match the overall direction of the market? When it comes to the stock market, you will find that it's either on an upward or downward spiral. You will want to match your trade with this direction.

Always Look at the Long-Term Charts

One of the biggest mistakes that beginner traders often make is that they will only focus on the short-term charts when they are looking into a stock. Many experienced traders feel that this is the wrong course of action as you should have a better idea of what the trend of the stock has done over at least a six-month period. Of course, you can always go longer than six months. You should start with the chart that will give you a couple of weeks. From there, you will want to make sure you go over the chart and notice every single detail. There is nothing that you should miss during the analysis of your chart. After you have looked at the first couple of weeks, then you can dive more into a long-term chart, such as the six-month chart. Again, follow the same microscopic process you did with the chart. Do your best not to miss anything. In fact, some traders will often create an excel spreadsheet where they can list everything they have to view in the chart and even write down information. This is a great piece of advice for any beginner.

Do Your Best Not to Enter Near the End of the Trade

Once you start to get into the stock market, you will notice a trend when it comes to traders. You will find that the stock market is busy within the first hour because there are so many traders who are buying new stocks for the day. You will then notice that the stock market begins to get quiet around the 11:00 hour because people are either holding on to their stocks or closed out for the day. However, about the last hour, which starts around 3:00 pm, you will notice the stock market picks up again as people, especially day traders, sell all their stocks and closeout.

As a swing trader, you might not buy and sell stocks every day. Unlike day traders, you can hold your stocks for a few days to about a week or two. However, there are a few traders that are not allowed to do this as it would cause them too much loss.

Another reason people enter into trades earlier rather than later is because this can give you the most profit, especially if you find a stock that is hitting an upward trend. On top of this, you will have less risk to worry about if you enter a trade early. Doing your best to cut down on risk is always something traders focus on, even if they don't mind taking risks.

Track a Consistent Group of Stocks

Just like every trader is different, every stock is different. This is why it is important to not focus on jumping from one stock to the next. Instead, as you are learning the tricks and strategies of swing trading, you will want to start getting an idea of what kind of stocks you like. Every stock has its own personality and once you catch on to that specific personality, trading will become easier if you stick to groups of stocks that are similar. One reason for this is because you will most likely be able to use the same strategy for all of your stocks. This can help you when it comes to learning techniques and strategies. It is easier to stick to one strategy because there are so many tiny details about swing trading you need to remember, the human brain can only hold determined information.

Another reason for this is because this allows you to be able to manage a certain amount of stocks consistently. If you are a full-time swing trader, you will find this system will give you less stress, keep your focus, and increase confidence in your abilities. Of course, all this will help you keep your right state of mind as a trader.

Always Have a Clear Plan

Whenever you enter a trade, you will want to make sure that you have a clear plan of action. This plan will most likely be your trading plan; however, this is known to change from time to time as traders start to learn and grow with their profession. While this is great as it means you are becoming a more successful trader, you will also want to make sure that you continue to update and adjust your plan as you need to.

Before you enter any trade, it is best to go through your plan and make sure that it will work with that stock. If you find it won't, then you will need to either adjust your trading plan or choose a stock that will fit your trading plan better.

You will want to make sure that everything is including in this plan from your entry to your exit. You will want to make sure that you have all the key points and details down. On top of this, you will also want to make sure that you have a stop-loss strategy in place so you can quickly let go of that stock through a trade and walk away from losing a large amount of money. Remember, when you decide the stop-loss strategy is the best course of action, it will happen quickly. In fact, trading is a very faced-paced business, which is another reason making sure you always have a clear plan of action is a commandment.

Always Integrate Fundamentals into Your Technical Analysis

One of the 11 commandments of swing trading is to make sure that you integrate fundamentals into your analysis. If you have looked into day trading, you will know a bit about fundamentals and more about technical analysis. However, when it comes to swing trading, fundamentals becomes just as important as technical analysis. The main reason for this is because you hold your stocks longer than a few minutes to a few hours.

Make Sure to Master the Psychological side of Swing Trading

There is a lot of psychology that goes into swing trading. In fact, psychology goes into any type of trading, but it is more crucial when it comes to swing traders. While part of this is about keeping the right mindset, the other part comes from the overall experience of swing trading. There are a lot of factors, such as making mistakes, learning, and losing that can affect your psyche throughout your day. For example, if you take a loss you might find that you feel like a failure after you have closed out your day. This can affect your personal life as well as your working life. It is extremely important to make sure that you have a healthy frame of mind and not just the right mindset when you are a trader.

Try Putting the Odds in Your Favor

Sometimes you will look at a trade and wonder if you will be able to make a profit on it. This is why it is important to use technical analysis with every trade. However, even if you feel that you might not be able to make a profit, this doesn't mean that you walk away from the trade. In fact, you can take this time to work on putting the odds in your favor. While this means you might end up risking a profit, trading is always full of risks. In fact, you will never be able to fully eliminate risks. Therefore, there are times where you have to take the leap and use certain techniques in order to try to work the trade into your favor.

Trade in Harmony with the Trend Time Frames

When it comes to the stock market, there are three types of trend time frames. The longest time frame is a year. The intermediate time frame is about three months. The shortest time frame is less than a month. When you are a swing trader, you will typically focus on the intermediate and short-term time frames. However, there are traders who have stated that they have looked at trends as far back as six months. Typically, swing traders don't have to focus on the longer time frame because they are considered to be short-term traders. At the same time, swing traders need to do more than just look at the short-term trend lines.

Make Sure to Use Multiple Indicators and Not Create Isolation

Sometimes traders will often feel that they only need to use one tool to give them an idea of what stock will give them a profitable trade and what stock won't. You should never do this. You always want to make sure that you use multiple tools and that these tools give you consistent results. For example, you might use a strategy, candlestick chart, volume, and other tools in order to find out that your trade will be profitable.

www.ingramcontent.com/pod-product-compliance
Lightning Source LLC
Chambersburg PA
CBHW061036050726
47592CB00004B/1466